The FIRST BOOK of

ANIMAL SIGNS

Written and illustrated by

C. B. Colby

Franklin Watts, Inc.
575 Lexington Avenue
New York, N.Y. 10022

Contents

Foreword

If you know what to look for and where to look, you can see many signs of human beings and of civilization, without ever seeing the people themselves. Even from a mountaintop or high-flying plane, you can see homes, cities, highways and signposts, plantings and harvestings. These are signs which tell you where people live and what they have been doing. A walk in the woods and fields is very much the same, for many signs of life and many kinds of activity are spread out before you.

One person might walk through a patch of woodland and see nothing. A trained outdoorsman might take the same walk and just by reading the signs about him find it teeming with all sorts of wildlife. It is a matter of being able to recognize animal signs and to interpret what they mean.

A sign might be a clump of leaves high in a leafless tree; a track in the dust at your feet; a pile of nutshells on a stump; or a few hairs caught in the pitch of a pine tree. To a naturalist each one tells a story about what is going on around him. If you learn to spot these signs and know their meaning, you can add tremendously to the pleasure of a weekend hike, a camping trip, or just a walk around your own garden or backyard.

If this book arouses your interest to look for animal signs, soon you will be able to recognize many of them for what they are, who made them, and perhaps you may learn something about the maker or builder.

The next time you go into the woods and fields, or even to a nearby park, take along a notebook — this book if you can — field glasses or binoculars, some curiosity, and a determination to know just who does live there. You may find that what you had thought was a deserted piece of landscape is really a teeming "Times Square" of animal activity. With practice you can become expert

iv

in reading animal signs, and the practice itself can be good fun even for those who have never tried it.

If practice does nothing more than make you really *see* what you have been only *looking at* before, I'll be delighted. Once you have learned to see the signs, I'm sure you will want to know about them. Then you will have already taken the first step in becoming a naturalist — something that will give you lifelong pleasure and constant challenges.

In selecting the subjects for *The First Book of Animal Signs,* I was guided by the kinds of animals that you would most likely find living near where you hike, camp, or spend a summer in the country. To include every animal sign that you might come across would require several books, especially since you will also find signs of birds, insects, and reptiles. Many of these creatures leave plenty of "signatures" around for you to see. So, if you find a sign that is not in this book, keep a record of your discovery for future solving and try to get to know the animal who made it. Your sign collection will then increase in fun as it increases in length.

In writing any book, an author usually has help from others, and *The First Book of Animal Signs* is no exception. I should like to thank the many fur-bearing helpers I had with this project, from Canada to Mexico and from Cape Breton to the western prairie, with a lot of stops in between. My special thanks to those who let me visit their homes, look at their feet, make sketches, take down their "conversation" on tape, and who generally allowed me to bother them in many ways. Thanks, too, even to those who frankly and noisily resented my intrusion into their private lives. Without their frequently unknowing cooperation, this book would have been much harder and a lot less fun to write and illustrate.

C.B.Colby

How to Use This Book

This book is arranged, not by animals, since you will probably not know what animal made the sign that you have found, but by *types* of signs. If you find a track, turn to the section on tracks, look for a similar track and check the size, general shape, and any outstanding characteristic, such as four toes, five toes, claw marks or no claw marks, shape of pads, etc. If these all match or nearly match, and it is reasonable to assume that such an animal is in the area, you have probably made a correct identification. The same procedure applies to identifying dens, burrows, droppings, or any of the other signs listed in the various sections. If you become familiar with the signs before you go looking for them, you will have a better idea of what to look for, and will be able to spot any signs that much easier. Practice makes perfect, and in this kind of nature study, practice also makes good fun.

Signs

Signs of animals may be anywhere and may be almost anything that is not "natural" in the woods. A sign might be a tuft of hair caught on a bush; the bark scraped from a tree; a gouge out of a bed of ferns; a track in the mud or dust; a flattened place in tall grass; or even a hole in the ice of a frozen swamp. All of these are made or put there by something alive.

Look carefully about you in the woods, and soon a great number of things will show that wildlife is all around you. Nature's creatures are a rather shy lot, and they prefer to watch you rather than to be watched themselves, but they cannot hide all their clues. These clues reveal their goings and comings, their hunting for food, their play, and even their tragedies.

Look for signs anywhere, high or low, or right at the toe of your boots. Look sharp and be curious about anything that does not look as if it grew, fell, or was blown there. One clue may lead to another, plainer one.

Some woodsmen say that winter is the easiest time to look for clues, but I feel that because there is a greater number of animals who roam about in the summer this makes up for the greater difficulty in finding their signs. It is just the personal preference of the naturalist. Both winter and summer have their own advantages. Tracks are easier to find, of course, in winter, but often harder to read with accuracy. On the other hand, in winter you can more easily follow a trail, which can be exciting. In summer there are more animals around, especially the smaller species which are probably close to your home, looking for food, raising families, and building homes.

So, regardless of the time of year, look closely about you as you cover the woods and fields. There is much to see, and for those who really look there is much to learn.

BLACK BEAR "NESTS" IN BEECH TREES

Black bears are extremely fond of beechnuts, those tiny, delicious, three-sided nuts that I used to hunt for as a youngster in New Hampshire. After cleaning up any nuts that are left on the ground by squirrels, the bear may climb a tree and shake down more of them.

Once the bear is in the tree, he will break off branches and make a crude platform to sit or sprawl upon while he enjoys his feast. As he breaks off a branch, he strips it of nuts and adds the wood to the pile under him. He may also break off boughs and take them back to his "nest" to eat the nuts at his leisure.

When you are in bear country and find a grove of beech trees, look into the branches above you for one or more of these platforms. In fall, after the leaves have dropped, they stand out like badly engineered crow's nests, a sure sign that black bears are, or have been, in the area.

BEAVER CUTTINGS

In beaver country, you may come across their cuttings some distance from their dams and houses. You will find stumps with tooth-marked tops; perhaps sections of logs with pointed ends or half-gnawed-through areas; and huge piles of chips. All of these are beaver signs.

Many beaver run out of suitable logs for either food or dam- and house-building, and so they travel some distance to obtain more. They frequently build canals from the new supply to their ponds, and float the logs and branches down the canals for storage until needed.

Many times I have seen spots in dirt roads near beaver ponds which look as though someone with a heavy, stiff broom has swept the road from side to side. This is where a beaver has dragged a branch or branches across the road to his pond.

Whenever you are in country where beaver are known to live, keep an eye out for any of these signs.

3

ELK MARKS ON ASPENS

Throughout the West, wherever aspen trees and elk are found, you can locate the elk's range by the distinctive marks that the big deer leave on the bark and trunks of these lovely trees.

The elk are particularly fond of aspen bark, and in winter it is their favorite food. Their broad teeth slice off the bark, right down to the bare wood, and their lower incisors leave deep grooves in the wood itself.

When the tree heals, the wood is rough and black. Often you will find groves of aspens with completely black trunks as high as an elk can reach. This marks a favorite feeding grove for many years.

In this sketch that I made in Wyoming, note the tooth marks on the aspen at the right, as well as the bark removed down to the wood. The tree at the left and those in the background show black healed areas from previous gnawings. Elk also eat the shoots and twigs of these trees, stripping them bare as high as they can reach. Sometimes they will stand on their hind legs to browse higher and higher up the trunks.

4

ANTLER VELVET

When any species of deer grows a new set of antlers, the antlers are covered at first with a very sensitive skin full of veins which feed the rapidly growing bone inside. Later, when the antlers are fully developed, this outer skin, or "velvet" as it is called, dies from lack of blood. It dries, splits, and itches, much like human skin after a bad sunburn. It is often seen hanging in strips and shreds from the antlers.

To remove this velvet, the animals rub their antlers on bushes, ledges, and tree trunks, scraping off the dead material in long scraps and strips. The dead material looks like shriveled-up pieces of rotted gray-green velvet, and it is quite brittle to handle if it has been there for some time. One side has a slightly fuzzy or "velvety" feel, while the other side feels a little like very old and thin parchment.

5

RABBIT GNAWINGS ON TREE BASES

During the winter months when the snows lie deep in the wilderness, small animals have a rough time finding food of any kind. Rabbits often resort to living on bark from the trunks of fruit trees.

If, after the snow has melted, you find fruit-tree trunks that are gouged and stripped of bark, you may be sure that there have been rabbits in the area.

Smaller animals, such as field mice, often do similar damage to small shrubs and bushes. This makes fruit farmers very unhappy because girdling the bark can easily kill the tree, even a good-sized one. If the tree has been completely stripped all around, it will die, but sometimes enough bark is left so that, in spite of extensive bleeding (loss of sap), the tree will heal itself and survive.

6

MINK TROUGHS, OR FURROWS, IN SNOW

When I first saw a mink trough many years ago, I thought it had been made by a huge snake or someone riding a bicycle with a big tire, for that is just what the mark in the snow looked like. Then I found out what really had made it — a mink.

This little member of the weasel family has very short legs, so that when the snow is deep, he may decide to "swim" through it instead of leaping across it. This method is not as fast but it takes less energy.

The mink simply stretches out his neck and chin and pushes with his feet, sliding through the snow like a black snowplow. The otter, another member of the weasel clan, also does this at times. If you follow one of these "tire marks" for any distance, eventually you will see the animal's footprints in the bottom of the trough. The footprints are about 3 or 4 inches wide and perhaps half as deep.

GNAWED ANTLERS

With all the deer in the world shedding their antlers every year, it is often a mystery why we are not up to our waists in old antlers. The reason we are not is because they are eaten!

This antler from a white-tailed deer was picked up while I was on an animal sound-taping trip to Ontario, Canada. I sketched it as it was found in wolf country. Wolves and small rodents had eaten all but the base of the antler, and they were still working on this, for it showed fresh tooth marks when I found it.

Many antlers are eaten each winter when they are shed (about the middle of February), by rodents who need the calcium that they contain. Not only rodents but ground squirrels, porcupines, and even deer and elk will gnaw cast-off antlers in this manner. Other antlers just fall apart over the years and add their materials to the soil.

Note in the sketch on this page how the powerful jaws of the wolves had crushed the main beam of the antler at the right, while the tooth marks of small rodents are also visible.

Look for these cast-off antlers along deer trails and near watering spots, as well as among the trees in old orchards where deer go to feed.

NUTSHELLS ON ROCKS

Frequently you will notice nutshells in little piles or groups on stone walls, rocks, or on logs. These are sure signs that squirrels have been about, dining on beechnuts, acorns, hickory nuts, and anything else in the nut family that they can find. Red, gray, and ground squirrels all love nuts.

Squirrels invariably carry their finds to the top of a rock or stump to eat, so they can keep an eye out for possible danger. And if they drop a nut it is easier to find on a rock than if they had dropped it in the leaves and ground rubbish of the forest floor.

If you want to be sure to find wildlife near your home or along your favorite woodland path, take along a pocketful of peanuts or other nuts, with shells or without, and leave a few on rocks that you can watch from a distance. Sunflower seeds, a favorite of chipmunks, may soon bring some of these little creatures right to your hand. Chipmunks live in my driveway stone wall, and after a few days of tempting them with these seeds, they lost all fear and were soon eating out of my hand so trustingly that I could stroke their sides.

9

ANTLER-RUBBED SHRUBS

You may have seen places on trees where two branches have rubbed together in high winds, so that the bark has been chafed away right down to the bare wood. But here are some branches where the bark has been worn away without the help of another branch.

This is a sign that there are deer in the area, especially some mature males, or bucks, with fine antlers.

When the antlers are fully developed, the bucks rub them on rocks, shrubs, and bushes to remove the "velvet." But once the velvet is gone, they rub the hardened antlers on sturdy shrubs to polish and sharpen the pointed tines. They also do this to learn just where the tines are and which way they are pointed, much as a fencer practices to learn where and how best to use his rapier or cutlass, for the bucks often use their antlers in deadly combat.

These trees, with the bark rubbed off and even the underbark scraped away to the white wood, can be found where any species of deer live and fight. Look for these telltale white areas on the brush from the end of summer until almost Christmas, or until the local mating season is over.

PORCUPINE DAMAGE TO TREES

The slow-moving porcupine, or "porky," can do more damage to a grove of fine timber than almost anything but a forest fire. He eats only the inner bark of such trees as birch, pine, maple, beech, spruce, and fir, and often spends several days in a single tree, eating and sleeping there without coming down.

Porcupines chip away the outer bark with their beaver-like teeth, and then cut off and eat the tasty inner bark, leaving the bare wood showing and often killing the trees by this girdling. These bare spots are usually just above the branch on which the animal has perched while eating.

At the base of such trees are great piles of the rough outer bark, droppings from the animal itself, and bits of twigs and cones that he has cut off to reach more of the trunk bark. If you notice such rubbish about the base of a tree, look up into the branches and you may see the culprit hard at work, stuffing himself with inner bark.

In the spring, the porky eats flowers and other vegetation, and, in summer, he eats vegetation, fruit, and leaves. But in the fall back he goes to the tall timber and his bark diet. Keep an eye out for his signs but if you see him do not touch him or go near enough for him to hit you with his stubby tail, for it is well armed with quills. He cannot, of course, shoot them, but he can certainly slap you with a tailful of quills faster than you can dodge.

TREES STRIPPED BY BEARS

Like most humans, bears have a sweet tooth. They will do anything to obtain honey, maple sap, or even the syrupy juice of evergreens that they find just under the outer bark.

If you are in the wilderness and come across a pine, fir, or spruce tree, with the bark ripped off from the ground to a height of several feet, you can be fairly sure that some roving bear has been using it for a candy cane. Look for deep claw-and-tooth gouges in the wood.

If you find such a tree stripped of its bark, but only up to a height of a couple of feet, the culprit was probably not a bear but a hungry snowshoe rabbit. Look for small tooth marks where the bark begins again. This will identify which one did the damage. Claw marks and big tooth marks indicate a bear, and tiny, cleancut tooth marks indicate a rabbit. Droppings nearby will also help to identify the proper animal.

DEER OR MOOSE BROWSE LINES

In the winter, when food is hard to find, deer or moose will eat the bark of many types of evergreens, gnawing it almost completely off for as high as they can reach. They also eat the twigs and tips.

I have seen areas in the wilderness that looked as if the trees had been scraped clean with special tools, right down to the bare wood. This is particularly true when a herd of deer has been forced by heavy snow to "yard up" in a grove of evergreens and cannot leave to seek food elsewhere.

In winter, the cause of the stripping is easy to determine for there will be tracks between the trees. But in summer it may look as though the tree has some strange disease. Watch for such stripped trees in deer or moose country as a sure sign that these big animals are about. Cedar trees, in particular, suffer from such stripping because their bark is a favorite of the white-tailed deer.

14

MUSKRAT BREATHER HOLES

Although most semiaquatic animals, such as mink, muskrat, and otter, who spend much of their time in or near the water, can stay under the surface of the water for a long while, they must all come up to breathe eventually.

This is somewhat of a problem when ice covers the pond in winter and the animal must go fishing for food. Various types of animals have solved this problem in their own ways. The muskrat has one of the most interesting solutions. He builds a special "breather hole" and uses wads of vegetation to keep it from freezing.

In this sketch I have moved the vegetation away to show the hole in the ice, but normally it would be covered and filled with grasses, roots, reed stalks, etc., sometimes to the size of a basketball. This plug keeps the hole from freezing solid, and when the swimmer has to have air he heads for one of these holes, pushes up through the plug of soft material, and gets his breath back.

Some of these breather-hole covers are so big that the muskrat can climb up into them for a rest, above the ice and yet out of sight. If danger does threaten, he can pop down through the hole again and return to his own home unseen.

If you find a frozen pond with muskrat houses, look for some of these little mounds of grasses and reeds.

RABBIT "FORMS"

Sometimes when you are walking through soft grass or near a thick clump of vegetation, you will note a depressed and matted nestlike spot. It may look as though something had been laying there for some time and was later taken away. The bits of grass or stalks may all be pushed down in one direction as though they had been arranged that way.

These small "nests" are made by rabbits and are called "forms" instead of nests or dens, for they are only favorite resting places of the little animals. Often they are used day after day if they give the user a feeling of security and offer him a good view of the area and some concealment from a possible enemy. They are frequently under a bush or overhanging ledge or small, low evergreen.

RED SQUIRREL CONE CACHES

It is said that when squirrels begin to store away food early in the fall, we are in for a long, hard winter. If that is true then almost any winter will be a rough one, for my backyard woodpile is usually crammed with pinecones which the local red squirrels stuff in between the logs.

Almost every space is jammed with cones to be hauled out later by the red squirrels when food is hard to find in other places. These cones are from white pine, Austrian pine, blue spruce, and hemlock, so the owners can have quite a variety of flavors to enjoy. Most of them are from my white pines.

Although there are few woodpiles in the wilderness, you may find such "pantries" among rocks, windfalls, and cracks in ledges. If you find pinecones any distance from a pine tree or in a place where they would not naturally fall or roll, you may be sure that there are red squirrels around, even if you cannot see or hear them. Almost any type of evergreen cone in such a place is a sign that it was put there by some small animal with an eye to a long, hard winter.

17

POCKET GOPHER TUNNELS

A few years ago, while camping at Jenny Lake, just north of Jackson Hole, Wyoming, I came across some odd-looking workings in the soil. One was a mound of dirt several inches across with a hole at one side of the mound which was plugged with a sort of ball of soft earth. A few feet away, I found another smaller ball. Under both were tunnel entrances. These were made by the little pocket gopher.

He digs his complicated tunnels and shoves the dirt out of the entrances and to one side. Then he shoves up enough loose dirt to plug the entrance, as shown in the sketch. If he makes another entrance nearby, he carts the dirt along the tunnel to the main entrance and then covers the second hole with a small plug of dirt. These caps of dirt are a sure sign of the pocket gopher.

During the winter he also digs new tunnels and shoves the loose dirt into tunnels under the snow where he has foraged for food. When the snow melts, these "snakes" of dirt are left just as they were packed into tunnels during his winter engineering.

If you examine closely the bases of bushes and tree trunks in the area, you will probably see where the pocket gopher has gnawed them during his winter-tunneling for food.

MINK AND WEASEL SNOW TUNNELS

Although the winter snows often cover up many signs of animal life in the woods, they also reveal many new signs. Tracks, in particular, are easy to find and follow, and much can be learned from following the trails as they wind through the brush and across the fields.

In this sketch you will see something you may have already noticed and wondered about — a sudden tunnel in the snow which interrupts a simple trail across a clearing.

Various types of weasels and mink often tunnel under the snow to look for field mice or other food. As they move across the snow they may hear or feel some slight movement underneath the surface. They promptly dive below to investigate, emerging some distance away to continue once more above the snow. Sometimes when snow covers tall grass or brush, it may give way beneath the animal, dumping him below the surface, but more often the tunnels are made in a deliberate search for food.

19

BOBCAT SCRATCHES ON TREES

If you have a cat at home, you know how he loves to sharpen his claws on furniture or shrubs. Perhaps you have a special post just for his use. Wild members of the cat family also do this to keep their claws in condition.

If you are in an area where bobcats, lynx, or mountain lions are found, look for these scratchings. The tree shown in the sketch is in New Hampshire. A bobcat had paused here to recondition his "weapons" before starting on a shopping trip into a big briar patch where rabbits came to feed.

Often you may notice scraps of bark at the base of such a tree. If you look closely at the bark, you can see where the claws have raked grooves in the wood.

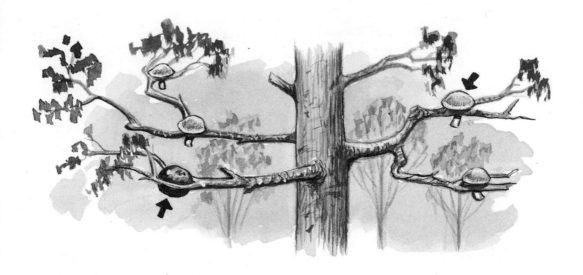

RED SQUIRREL "MUSHROOM TREES"

We all know that mushrooms do not grow on trees, so if you ever find them in trees in the woods, you can be sure that they had some help getting there. That help was probably the handiwork of a red squirrel who not only likes mushrooms but likes to store them away for future use. He also stores fruit in this manner.

Like all small animals, red squirrels have an instinctive urge to hoard food for the future. They frequently forget where they hid such treasures, but nevertheless they keep right on hiding things. Many of our forest trees grew from seeds and nuts hidden years ago by absentminded squirrels.

If you see anything hanging from the crotch of a bush or tree, make a note of it and check back later to see if the hoarder has returned to collect his treasure.

BEAVER "MUD PIES"

If you are ever in beaver country, you may come across some peculiar little piles of what look like small mud pies. They may be on rocks out in the water, or in certain spots on the shore of a pond or lake.

There is a strong pungent odor about these little pie piles, and for a very good reason. These "pies" mark the boundary of the beaver's "property," and they advertise that the male beaver is interested in meeting a female beaver. Some of the piles may be 3 feet in diameter and 1 foot high; others are not much more than a little mud-daubed grass or a few reeds bent together and held with mud.

Once the beaver has constructed a pie, he sprinkles it with a liquid from a gland near his tail. The liquid is called castoreum, or beaver scent, and it is much like, but less offensive than, the liquid used by a skunk for defense. Castoreum apparently holds great attraction for other beaver, as well as for some animals of other species, for northern woodsmen often use a few drops of it to lure animals to their traps.

RABBIT SNIPPINGS OF EVERGREENS

Keen eyesight will often show you where a rabbit has had his lunch. If you spot tips of evergreens which have been neatly snipped off close to the branch, you can be sure that rabbits have been on a shopping trip.

If the snipped branches are close to the ground, this might also be the work of a grouse, but more likely a rabbit has been there. You might have to lift the ends of the branches to examine them closely enough to find these clippings.

ROTTEN LOGS RIPPED OPEN BY BEARS

When you are looking for animal signs in the woods, you must play a sort of detective game in order to recognize the signs when you find them.

For example, if you find a log such as the one I have sketched from a photo that I took in the Catskill Mountains a few years ago, look at it closely. If the wood from the hole in the top has fallen down into the log, it was caused by natural rotting and the force of gravity. On the other hand, if the wood from the top has been pulled away and tossed aside, as in the sketch, a bear has probably been investigating the interior for grubs and termites.

If you look closely at the edges of the opening and the discarded pieces, you may see tooth or claw marks: confirmation that bruin has been at work. Check the interior of the log for signs of termites, honeycombed wood, and portions ripped away — still more proof of a visiting bear.

24

GAME TRAILS TO WATERING PLACES

Wildlife always seem to have a favorite place when they go to drink, and eventually the daily traffic will wear down an obvious trail to the water's edge.

The trail is often on some little point of land where the water can be reached easily without climbing down a bank. When an animal is drinking, he naturally has his head down, so he is vulnerable to attack from behind and to the sides. Therefore he chooses a drinking spot where he can eliminate attack from most directions.

The trail I have sketched is within a couple of miles of my home and is used by deer, often several at one time. If you discover one of these little trails to a "drinking fountain," you might find it a fine place to observe wildlife.

Test the wind and select a spot a few yards away from the site on the downwind side, so that the wind blows from the spot to you. This keeps your scent from any animal who comes there. Animals usually drink early in the morning and in late afternoon, so get to your observation post before those times and keep very still.

DEER TRAILS IN LEAVES

When a blanket of leaves covers the forest floor, it usually covers all the tracks which were there, but sometimes it helps to find them.

In the fall, when the bucks of the deer family are proudly stalking the wilderness with fine antlers on their heads, they have a habit of dragging their feet as they swagger about. This produces a very definite trail in deep leaves, which can be seen quite easily. During the early morning and late afternoon, when the sun is low and the shadows long, these trails show up the best. This is particularly true in open woodlands, as in the sketch.

Does, unlike their mates, are comparatively dainty walkers and do not, as a rule, leave such trails. Other animals occasionally leave trails in the leaves as they pass, but they are not as well defined as those of the big male deer.

FOX DIGGINGS FOR GRUBS

All members of the canine family, dogs and their relatives, are fine
diggers, whether digging a den, burying a bone, or uncovering a
choice field mouse.

The fox is no exception, and you can quite easily tell his distinctive diggings in the fields and woodlands: they are almost always
rectangular in shape and about 3 inches deep. The fox digs with
his front feet in alternate motions as he looks for grubs under the
sod. Note the discarded dirt in the sketch.

It is impossible to tell from a particular "dig" just what kind of
fox made it, but if you know what species lives in the area you can
pretty well guess. But just noticing such a dig will tell you that a
fox is somewhere around. Compare this type of dig with that made
by a skunk, page 28.

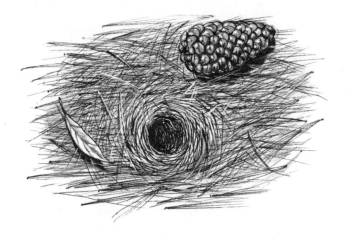

SKUNK DIGGINGS FOR GRUBS

Perhaps you have noticed small round holes in your yard or lawn, or in fields near your home. These are signs left by skunks as they dig for grubs or worms just below the surface. They are usually made during the nighttime.

The holes are almost round in shape with little or no dirt pulled out of the opening, in contrast to the grub diggings of the fox. If you find one of these skunk workings in pine needles, as I have sketched, you will notice that the animal used his agile front paws to work the needles away from the spot in an almost spiral pattern. The needles away from the rim of the hole have hardly been disturbed.

These diggings are evidence that skunks are finding and eating grubs which often do great damage to a lawn or to vegetation. When you discover such holes in your lawn, you can thank the small black-and-white sentry for working on a problem that you probably did not even know you had.

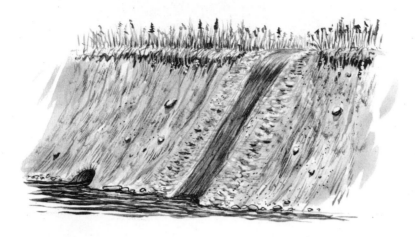

OTTER SLIDES

For the most fun-loving character in the wilds, the river otter takes the blue ribbon, hands (or paws) down. Otters will stop anything they are doing for a roughhouse, or a belly whop down a bank slide into the water.

In the winter they slide down snowbanks and scoot across bare ice for hours on end, apparently for the fun of it. You can find these slides in otter country both winter and summer. The summer slides are worn slick and smooth by the wet fur of the animals as they race up the bank only to come shooting down again. In winter the snow slides may be 15 or 20 feet long, and sometimes they end up on smooth ice so that the animal can keep right on sliding. Both old and young otters take part in this bobsledding. With their front paws against their sides and their hind legs trailing behind, their long tails following every undulation in the slide, they come zipping down just as you do on a slide in a carnival fun house!

Look for these slides along riverbanks in otter country, and if you see a family in action, it will be a rare treat.

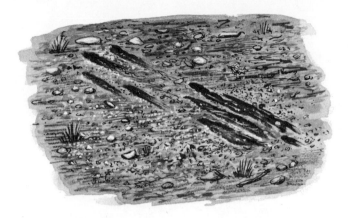

WOLF SCRATCHINGS

Like all dogs, the wild wolf loves to scratch and dig with his paws. When he is nervous, frightened, or uncertain, he will scratch apparently just to relieve tension.

Several times while I was following a wolf trapper as he checked his traps in Ontario, Canada, he pointed out where a wolf, scenting a trap nearby, had dug deeply into the ground with his paws in nervousness. The scratchings in this sketch had been made just a few moments before we arrived.

Wolves also scratch to cover their droppings as dogs do, merely throwing some dirt with their paws. The nervous scratching seems to have no purpose except to show the wolf's irritation at something he cannot understand — the scent of a trap nearby; its strong bait; man or vehicle tracks — or perhaps because he suspects that something is not quite normal in "his" woods.

If you are ever on an old logging road in the wilderness, far from where a domestic dog might be found, and you see these scratchings, you can be pretty certain that you are in wolf country. You might even find such marks near your camp or along riverbanks where the ground is clear.

FIELD MICE TUNNELS REVEALED BY THAW

When the snow is deep there often seems to be a complete lack of wildlife activity, but this is far from the truth. Down below the snow, life goes on pretty much as usual for many small animals such as the field or meadow mouse and his related species, all called voles. They are about the size of a house mouse but have shorter tails.

In the summer, they build miles of tiny tunnels in the grass, and when winter brings snow, they just keep right on building tunnels under the snow. These tunnels connect dens with many storage spots for food. When the snow thaws in spring or during warm spells, many of these wandering tunnels are exposed, revealing, as shown in the sketch, where the small creatures have been scooting around under the snow looking for food. If you have a large backyard or can visit one in the early spring, look for these tunnels when the snow is almost gone.

BEAVER DAMS

Practically any nature lover knows what this sketch is — a beaver dam. I drew this one in the beautiful Mont Tremblant Park in Quebec, Canada, where I have camped many times.

Some of these dams are strong enough and wide enough to drive a small truck across them, and when they have to be removed it takes several sticks of dynamite to break them down. They are made of logs, sticks, stones, and mud.

The dams are built by colonies of beaver to keep the water level around their big dome-roofed homes at a constant level. Any change in this water level is noticed at once, and the animals hurry to the dam to either let water out or to repair any leaks.

When you spot a beaver dam, there will be no question as to what it is. If at all possible go over to it and examine it closely, for it is a marvel of engineering, and perhaps you might even see one of the engineers at work.

TRACKS AFTER THAW

Frequently in spring after a thaw you may find a long row of small flat-topped "plateaus" crossing a field or clearing. These little frozen "pegs" are what were once animal tracks. When the animal's feet pressed the snow down as he walked across the field, the pressure compacted the snow so that it melted slower than the soft snow around it. The tracks remain like little stubby posts of hard snow when the rest of the snow melts away.

It is difficult to tell what animal made these plateaus except by the size and placement of the feet. If the pegs are pointed and all the points are on the same side of the peg, they were probably made by a deer. If they are rounded and in a straight line, they could be fox tracks (if fox are in the area), and if they are quite small and round they might be the tracks of a bobcat.

It takes a fairly heavy animal to compact the snow enough to form these little raised signs, so bear this in mind when you are trying to figure out what made them.

Tracks

An animal will leave some sort of track almost wherever he walks. Although the tracks are rarely perfect, there is usually enough detail among several of them to piece together what a whole one looks like, in order to identify the species. Once you identify a rabbit, deer, bear, or cat track, you will never mistake it for that of another species.

Although several animals leave tracks that are similar in general outline (large coyote and small wolf; mule deer and white-tailed deer; lynx and mountain lion, etc.), if you know what animal *might* be in the area, it will help you to pinpoint the probable track maker. No one would expect to find a mule deer in New Hampshire, so any deer track found there would undoubtedly be that of the white-tailed deer. Or a cloven-hoof track in Arizona would hardly belong to a tundra-living caribou. On the other hand, a "lynx" track in New Mexico would more likely be that of a mountain lion.

It is almost impossible to show what a perfect "typical" track for any particular species looks like, for the tracks vary in size, surface upon which they are made, and speed of the animal. Tracks even vary between animals of the same species. Therefore, I have sketched these tracks, based upon many years of observation, including the characteristics of the tracks of each species. I have studied the feet (alive and kicking, literally) of many species, and made plaster casts of numerous tracks in the woods where I found them.

Depending upon where you live, hike, camp, or travel, you may or may not find some of these tracks which I have included. Or you may find some that I have omitted for lack of space. For example, I have left out the tracks of such small creatures as field mice, some of the weasels, and one or two others, for they are either so tiny that their tracks are almost impossible to find, or so rare that their tracks are seldom seen. Some tracks are so close to each other in detail that it would be practically impossible to tell who made what without seeing the actual animal as he made them; as, for instance, the black-tailed deer and the mule deer.

Animals who are mainly tree dwellers — squirrels, raccoons, etc. — rather than strictly ground-living animals — deer, fox — bound along, placing their feet side by side on the ground with each bound. The hind feet, which strike the ground after the front feet, hit the ground beyond the marks left by the front feet.

Ground dwelling animals, who are not agile climbers, strike the ground with their front feet placed diagonally, one ahead of the other, at each bound. The hind feet, like those of the climbers, hit the ground beyond the marks of the front feet.

Finding the answer to "Who went there?" can be as exciting as finding the original animal in the woods. Make careful sketches of any strange tracks that you find, for the chances are that sooner or later you will see the animal who made them, either in his own habitat, in a zoo, or in a book on animals.

If you see an animal in the wilds, look at once for his tracks and study them well. Then the next time you find those tracks you'll know immediately who made them.

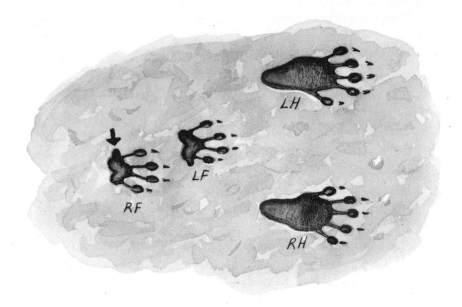

CHIPMUNK

It will be a challenge for you to find these dainty little tracks, for they are hardly 1 inch long for the hind feet and less than ½ inch long for the front feet. These are the tracks of the little eastern chipmunk, the most abundant of the several species of these friendly little rodents.

As you can see from the diagonal placement of the front feet, this animal is more used to ground travel than to climbing, although he can scamper up a tree if he needs to.

There are five toes on the hind feet and four on the front feet, plus a little pink "thumb" indicated by the arrow. The thumb is used for holding nuts and other foods for eating. Look for these tracks around pine trees and seed-bearing plants where there is fine soft dust, or in fresh mud near where the animals feed.

36

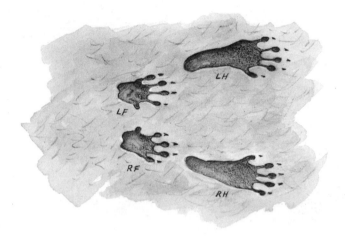

RED SQUIRREL

The tracks of the noisy red squirrel are similar to those of the chip-munk except that they are larger, measuring about 1¾ inches for the hind feet and about ¾ inch for the front paws.

From the placement of the front feet when the animal is bound-ing, as I have sketched, in a side by side position, you will know that this is a climbing animal. He sleeps only during the coldest and most stormy days, so you may find his tracks in the snow almost any day of the winter. Unlike the chipmunk, the red squirrel does not hibernate, and can be seen all year round.

Look for his tracks around favorite stumps where he goes to feed, and in fresh snow where he has walked between trees that are too far apart for him to travel through the branches. In sum-mer, the tracks might be found in soft dust near favorite nut trees or eating places. Squirrels are such light animals that they make very light tracks in only the softest dust.

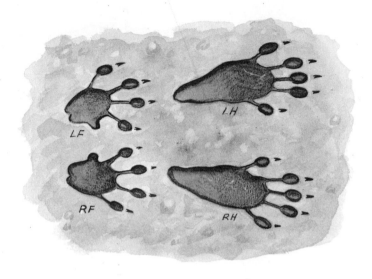

GRAY SQUIRREL

The gray squirrel and his western relatives have much larger feet than either the chipmunk or the red squirrel. They measure about 2½ inches long for the hind feet and over 1 inch for the front feet. Since the gray squirrel is a climbing animal, the front feet are placed side by side when bounding.

The "gray" squirrel may also be dark brown or completely black, and occasionally white. (I have a most unusual mounted specimen which is completely black with the exception of his tail tip which is snow-white. He was a traffic casualty on one of our local roads.)

Look for tracks of the gray squirrel near cone-bearing trees or in snow, as he does not hibernate except in very bad weather. He will get into attics if he can. If you have gray squirrels in your attic, you may find his tracks in the dust near his entrance, by a pipe, ventilator, or window.

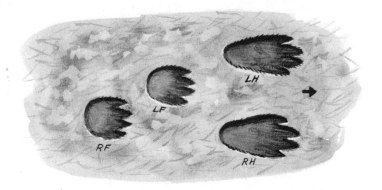

COTTONTAIL RABBIT

Almost anywhere that there is snow and a briar patch, you can find the tracks of the cottontail. This little rabbit is found over most of the country from the open woodlands right up to intown back doors, and into Canada, Mexico, and Central America.

The cottontail has pads on his toes, but they almost never show in the tracks because of the fur on the bottoms of all his feet. The tracks are actually hardly more than smudges in snow or dirt, but occasionally the claw marks will show at the front of the tracks, when the rabbit has skidded in mud or soft dirt.

Both hares and rabbits have five toes on the front feet and four on the hind feet, but only four toes show on either front or back feet except under most unusual circumstances. The tracks of the hind feet are about 3 inches long, while those of the front feet are hardly more than 1 inch in length. The toes are not always separated as shown here.

Rabbits are a "bounder" type of animal, so the tracks of the front feet appear behind those of the back feet because they strike the ground first, as shown in the sketch. The toe marks always point in the direction of travel (arrow).

39

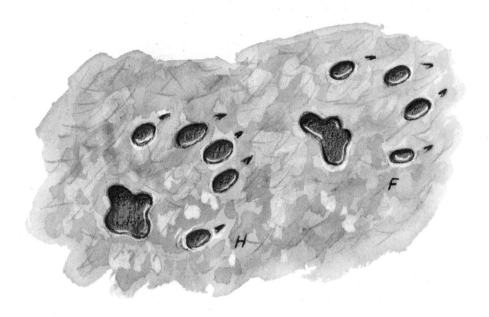

WOODCHUCK

The tracks of the eastern woodchuck may be found in gardens, bare spots in clover patches, and around the entrance of his den in the excavated dirt from the tunnel to his burrow.

They measure about 1½ inches long, and the front-paw track shows the mark of four toes and the palm pad, while the hind-foot track shows the imprint of five toes and the heel pad. Note the difference between the palm and heel pads. Most tracks show the difference between these pads in practically all animals. The toes are quite small and well spaced in the tracks.

The tracks of the hoary marmot, a larger close relative, are found in the western portions of the United States. They are very similar to the tracks of the woodchuck except that the heel pads of the hind feet may be a bit longer and extend farther to the rear.

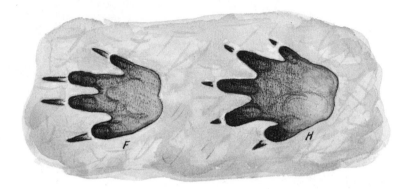

ARMADILLO

Throughout the Southwest and in some portions of Florida, the odd tracks of the armadillo can be found in the dust of the roadside or in the muddy banks of waterholes or streams where the animal goes to bathe or drink. They are also thick about the armadillo's den or burrow.

These armored creatures have curious, lizard-like feet with four toes on the front and five on the hind, each equipped with a long strong claw for digging. The bottoms of the armadillo's feet are strongly padded and muscular, although this does not show in his tracks as he shuffles along.

The front feet make tracks about 2¼ inches long; the hind feet are a bit shorter. The claws on the front feet are longer than those of the back feet and they make powerful digging tools. The armadillo lives in a burrow and his well-worn trails lead from there in all directions to favorite eating and drinking spots.

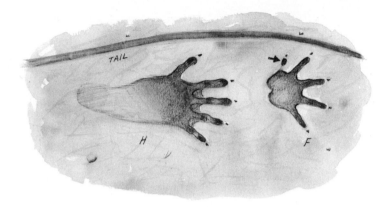

MUSKRAT

In the soft mud of marsh and swamp edges, or along the snowy rims of these places in winter, you may find the tracks of the muskrat. This water rat is said to walk on the entire flat of his hind feet, but he actually steps more heavily on the toes of his rear feet. This makes the front of the hind-feet track more deeply imprinted, as I have sketched.

There are five toes on both front and hind feet, but the fourth toe on the front feet is so tiny that it rarely shows at all in a track. This is called the inner toe, and as you can see in the sketch (arrow), it is almost nonexistent. The muskrat's partially webbed hind feet leave quite a broad track. The claws are fairly small. The track of the hind foot averages about 3½ inches long and the front foot about 1⅛ inches long.

The tracks of the muskrat are seldom found any great distance from water or wetlands, but since he is active all year long, you can look for his tracks anytime you are near where he lives. The drag mark of his tail is often seen as a wavy mark between the right and left legs as the animal moves along. In snow this is particularly easy to spot.

BEAVER

It is rare to find a good example of beaver tracks, for the beaver spends much of his time in water, and on dry land his broad, scaly tail drags over the tracks and usually erases them. However, if you do find a broad-webbed track, or part of one, you may be sure it is that of the beaver.

The front foot of the beaver has five toes, but usually only three or four toes register. The wide hind foot has five toes but generally the second claw does not register. This is a split claw and may be used as a comb for grooming.

The length of the huge hind feet of the beaver is about 6½ or more inches long, while the front feet measure about half this length.

Look for beaver tracks along the banks of beaver ponds, near their dams and canals, and also near where they have been cutting trees. However, if they are "logging" and dragging branches behind them, their tracks will be erased by the brush. You may also find their tracks on shores where they have erected their "mud pie" markers.

43

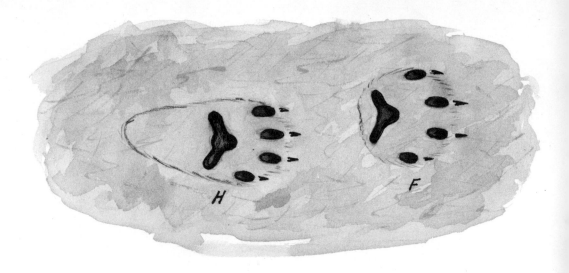

WEASEL

The tracks of the weasel vary with the size and species, but the common weasel's tracks measure about 1⅛ inches for the front feet and up to 1½ inches for the entire hind foot.

The track of the hind feet may only show the toe and heel pads, as I have sketched. If the track is in snow or soft earth or mud, the entire bottom of the foot may be shown, as lightly indicated. Both front and hind feet have five toes, but the tracks show only four. When this little animal bounds along, the tracks may be about 20 inches apart and in pairs, with a slight mark of the tail drag between the opposite set of feet. When the weasel is in a hurry, he can cover as much as 6 feet in one leap, and when he is bounding along, his hind feet land in the tracks of his front feet, so separate tracks are hard to find.

Look for weasel tracks near where field mice are found, along brook and lake shores, and near chicken houses.

44

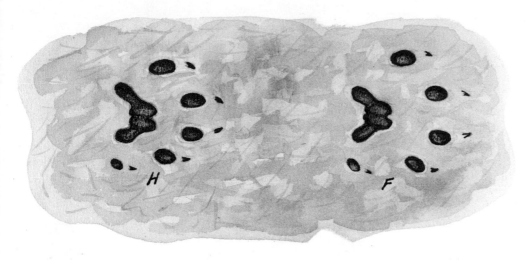

MINK

Although the mink is a hard-to-find creature, he leaves his tracks in many places that you might least expect. I have seen mink along a small brook near my home, and once a friend of mine found one in her kitchen battling her cat for his fish dinner. The tracks are usually found along stream and marsh banks where mink hunt for food, and near their homes under the banks.

There are five toes on each foot but usually only the four larger toes register in the track. If the little animal is scrambling up a bank or skidding in soft mud, you might find all five claw-and-toe marks. The front feet measure about 1⅜ inches in length; the hind feet are a trifle smaller. This animal bounds along in a sort of rippling gait, leaving four prints of his paws, then a space, and four more imprints. There may also be a tail-drag mark near where he lands after a bound. The bounds may cover a foot or two at a time and, as with all bounding animals, the tracks of the hind feet are before those of the front feet.

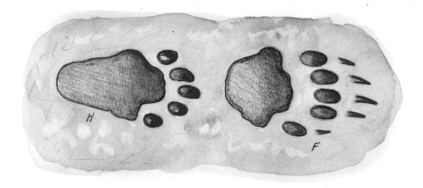

BADGER

Throughout the entire western portion of the United States and in the East just below the Great Lakes, this large member of the weasel family leaves his tracks. The badger is a great digger, so his front paws are equipped with long and powerful claws. These show in his tracks, while the smaller claws of his hind feet are seldom seen in tracks at all. There are five toes and five claws on each foot, and his tracks closely resemble those of various skunks, also members of the weasel clan.

The front feet of the badger measure about 3½ inches long, while his hind feet, because of the lack of long claws, are slightly shorter. When the badger walks, he sort of shuffles along with the tracks close together. The feet toe in slightly like those of many skunks.

Look for the tracks of the badger near his den or burrow, and around the burrows of other smaller animals, which he has dug up for food.

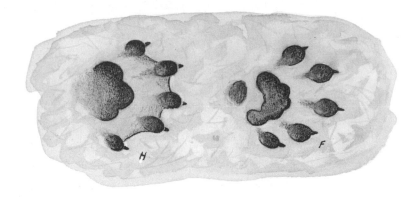

OTTER

This big member of the weasel family can be found from northern Canada down to southern South America, in one species or another. The Canadian, common, or river otter is most common to Canada and the United States.

Although the otter spends much of his time in or very close to water, he may travel many miles cross-country in winter looking for open water in which to fish. He travels in a series of bounds, as his legs are short. You can easily follow the trail in the snow. The feet have five toes on each foot and generally all five register. The long, heavy, tapered tail also leaves a mark in the snow.

The length of the hind feet is about 2½ inches; the front feet are a bit smaller. The impression of the track is generally round. When the otter travels through snow, he leaves a furrow similar to that of the mink, with the tracks in the bottom of the furrow. At other times he bounds along with his feet in a group at the end of each bound, and the mark of the tail shows plainly.

These tracks may be spotted along river, pond, and stream banks, near otter dens and slides, and sometimes quite a distance from water if the animal is on an overland hunting safari to new lands for food or a mate.

47

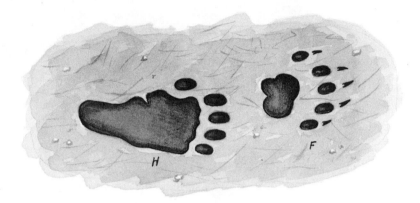

STRIPED SKUNK

Although there are several species of skunks — striped, spotted, hog-nosed, etc. — they all have similar tracks with five toes showing in both tracks of the front feet and the hind feet.

The claws of the hind feet are used for digging and rarely show. They are quite short, as compared to the front feet, which are fairly wide with large palm pads. The tracks of the hind feet reveal that skunks are plantigrades; that is, they walk on the entire sole of the hind feet and not on just the toes. This is true of many other animals, as you can see from their tracks.

You can find skunk tracks near garbage pails in the country, in chicken houses and barnyards, and along the dusty sides of country roads. If you find tracks that look like this sketch, check for long heel pads, the lack of claw marks on the hind feet, and wide, five-toed front feet.

Adult skunk tracks measure about 1¾ inches for the front feet and about 2½ inches for the hind feet.

OPOSSUM

These odd handlike tracks belong to the opossum. They are unusual in that the "thumb" of the hind foot has no claw (arrow). This animal, a sort of leftover from prehistoric times, is nocturnal and seldom seen in daylight.

Occasionally I have seen one at night on my feeding stations for raccoons. Opossums are quite slow-moving and apparently not particularly afraid of man, or else they are too slow-witted to be frightened. I can walk right up to one and lift it by the tail to look at its feet, as long as I keep a flashlight beam on its face.

The tracks measure about 1¾ inches long and frequently can be found along stream banks and, near civilization, around garbage pails and dumps. The opossum, which was originally found only in the warm southlands, has now extended his range to include much of New England, practically all of the Midwest, and into California.

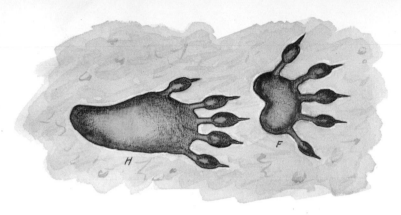

RACCOON

Many a suburban homeowner has found these tracks around his garden or garbage pail, especially after the pail has been tipped over and the contents scattered about the yard. Tracks from wet garbage may even enter his garage or climb his porch steps, for the raccoon is an inquisitive and neighborly sort of chap who always likes to look things over during the night.

These tracks measure about 4½ inches in length for the hind feet and about half that for the front feet or paws. I call them "paws" because they are more than just feet to walk on. The raccoon can untie knots like a Boy Scout, slide bolts like a safe-cracker, and generally do things with his paws that would make a magician envious. He is one of the most intelligent and adaptable creatures in the wilds. He can live with man and like it, even if the man, on the other hand, does not share his enthusiasm. I've been friends with raccoon families for years.

The raccoon is a plantigrade and walks on the whole sole of his hind feet. He is an expert tree climber, so when he bounds along, his front feet are paired side by side like those of the squirrel, with the hind feet landing beyond the front, ready for the next bound.

You may find these tracks along stream and pond banks, near his den trees, and in snow; almost anywhere that there are things to eat and tamper with in raccoon country.

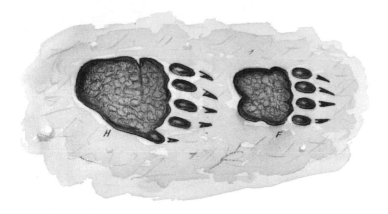

PORCUPINE

If you are in woods where there are porcupines at work, you will be able to spot their tracks around the trees they have climbed to enjoy a meal of bark. If you see these slow-witted animals in a tree, and if there is snow on the ground but no tracks about the tree, you will know that they have been up there since before the last storm, perhaps for several days. These animals have long claws on all feet and there are four toes on the front feet and five on the hind feet. The tracks also show, if they are clear and sharp, the heavily callused soles of the feet. This gives the track surface a sort of "pebbled" appearance. The length of the tracks are about 4 inches for the front feet and 4½ inches for the hind feet.

When he walks, the porcupine waddles with his feet toeing in, and when he does bound along, which is rare, his feet are paired like those of all climbing animals. In snow, he leaves a deep furrow, but his heavy tail may eliminate the tracks as it is dragged over them.

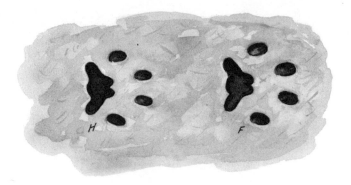

BOBCAT

One of the most dainty and most difficult tracks to find in the woods are those of the bobcat. This elusive wild feline is seldom seen.

He is found over most of the country and into Canada, where his larger relative, the Canada lynx, lives. The tracks are very similar except that those of the lynx are about 3 inches long compared with the 2-inch track of the smaller bobcat, sometimes called the bay lynx.

The toe pads of the bobcat are smaller than those of the lynx, but each animal has five toes on each foot. Being felines, the toes have fully retractile claws (meaning that they can pull them in) so they do not show in the tracks. Both of these cats can leap as much as 15 feet. (The tracks of the mountain lion are also similar, but are 3½ inches long.) Watch for bobcat tracks in real wilderness areas or in very rocky places even fairly close to civilization. I have found them about 60 miles from New York City.

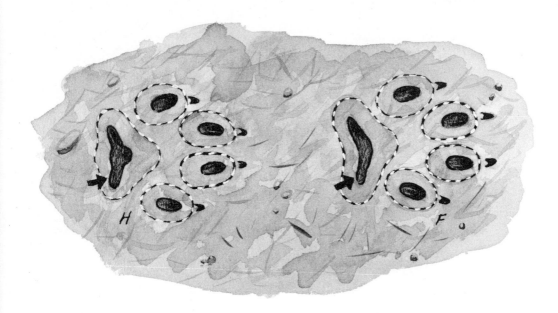

RED FOX

You will notice that I have shown these tracks in dotted as well as solid lines. The reason for this is that the red fox has a very odd foot. The pads are partially covered with hair so that usually only the bare portions of the pads leave a mark. I have shown in dotted lines the true size and outline of the red fox track. The solid dark areas are the portions that usually make the track, unless the ground is soft or covered with snow.

You can see that only the centers of the heel and palm pads make tracks, and that is because there is a small ridge across both of these pads from side to side (arrows). These ridges touch the ground before the whole pads do. The tracks measure about 2¼ inches long. Tracks of other species of fox are about the same size.

Look for fox tracks in soft dirt near their dens or burrows, around chicken houses, and in mud where they go to drink.

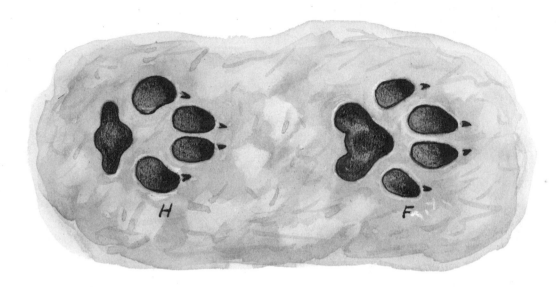

COYOTE

The tracks of the coyote can be found throughout the West, and more and more frequently in the East as well, for this animal has extended his original range. He is now found even in many areas of New England, as well as in upper New York State.

The tracks are doglike and measure about 3¼ inches long. Note the difference between the palm pads and the heel pads. Frequently the outer toe pads of the hind feet are larger than the inner toes, a typical coyote track characteristic. There are four toes on each foot, and being canines, the toes all show in the tracks, just as in the tracks of other canines, the fox and wolf.

Look for coyote tracks among the sagebrush where he hunts for jackrabbits, in the dirt near his den, and where he goes to drink.

54

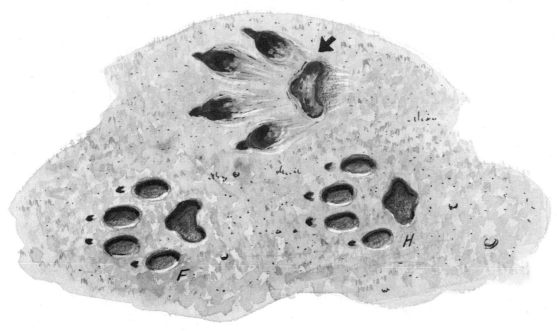

WOLF

The first time that you look down and see a wolf track beside your own boot, it may seem too huge to be real. Some wolf tracks measure as much as 6 inches long, especially when the wolf was speeding and the toes were spread in soft mud (arrow). Compare the size of these tracks with those of a dog and you will see just how enormous a wolf's track can be.

The timber wolf, or gray wolf, is the most common and can be found in some of our northern midwestern states, such as Michigan and Wisconsin, as well as in Canada. I sketched these in Ontario, Canada. Originally, wolves were found over most of the United States.

Look for the tracks along logging roads, near the wolf's den or burrow, and where he has gone to a stream or pond to drink.

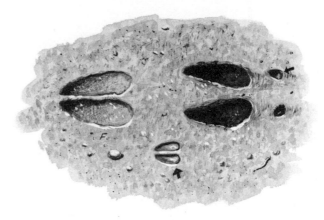

DEER

Even before the Pilgrims landed on our shores, the members of the deer family were an important source of meat. Today the tracks of the white-tailed deer can be found practically from coast to coast and into Canada.

The tracks are heart shaped or "arrowhead" shaped, and those of the bucks measure about 3 inches long. Doe tracks are slightly smaller and the tracks of the little fawns look like those of a toy. When a big deer is speeding and the ground is soft, the sections of the hooves will spread and the points of the dewclaws will also make tracks. The darker track at right shows the track of a speeding buck; note the marks of dewclaws and spread main sections. Arrows point (right) to dewclaw mark; and (left) to fawn.

In the West, the mule deer and the coast black-tailed deer replace the white-tailed deer, and they make almost identical tracks. The track of the moose is much heavier and larger — 7 inches or more. Look for any of these tracks in evergreen groves in winter and almost anywhere in deer country in summer, for deer move about constantly in search of food. Orchards are favorite places for deer, so check there as well as where they go to drink.

CARIBOU

The tracks of the caribou show how Nature adapts her children's feet to their particular type of problem. Since this large deer must walk on spongy muskeg (thick vegetable matter), snow, and ice, several factors in his hooves make travel easier. The caribou has especially long dewclaws to reach the ground and to help support the animal's weight, somewhat like the high heels on a woman's shoe. This helps on the mushy muskeg and on snow. The inner parts of the hooves dry up, leaving the hard outer edges to act as "skates," so the animal can walk quite securely on ice. The general round shape helps to prevent sinking in soft surfaces, as small snowshoes would do.

These hooves, which I sketched in Saskatchewan, are about 7½ inches, including the dewclaws. Caribou tracks will be found in northern Canada.

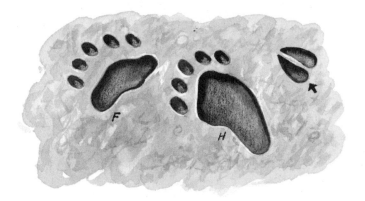

BLACK BEAR

Once found over practically all of the United States, the black bear is now limited to the wilder areas, but he is still plentiful. These tracks were sketched less than 150 miles from New York City, in the Catskill Mountains.

Although a black bear can climb a tree with speed and ease, his claws do not usually show in his tracks. Often just faint imprints of the claw tips can be found if the animal walks in mud or soft snow. The hind-feet tracks measure about 6 inches long, while those of the front feet are a bit shorter. Some tracks are even larger.

You can find black-bear tracks in old orchards, near "bee trees" or rotted logs which might contain ants and termites, and around wild berry patches. Since he is a plantigrade, the entire soles of his hind feet register when he walks. The fifth toes frequently do not register at all, although they are well developed.

For comparison, I have sketched a deer track alongside the hind foot of the bear, so you can see how big the black bear's feet really are.

Dens, Houses, and Homes

All but a few species of animals use some sort of den, burrow, home, house, or shelter. Being able to identify them and their owners can tell you what sort of animal homemakers live around you in the woods and fields.

Some animals live in holes in trees, some in burrows in the ground, and some in dens among the rocks. Others build elaborate houses of sticks, mud, grasses or reeds. Some take over the abandoned homes of others and rebuild them to suit their own tastes. There are many very clever architects in the wilderness.

Where to look for these residences and how to tell who lives there is an interesting part of learning and recognizing animal signs. Some dwellings are small and hard to find; others are large enough to climb on and even enter, if you know where the door is. A chipmunk or meadow vole can dart in and out of a hole the size of a quarter, while a beaver's house or grizzly den may be large enough to hold a barbershop quartet.

Look for openings in sunny meadow slopes, trees, stone walls, logs, ledges, stream banks, or between the roots of trees and stumps. Look for trails leading to such entrances. Look into high branches for nests, into tall grass for beds and "forms," and into marshes for houses of sticks and bulrushes. Check the doorways of these structures and dens for tracks, meal leftovers, bits of fur, bones, and feathers, to give clues as to whom the owner might be. Compare what you find with the sketches in this book and you will soon be able to tell a lot about who might be at home inside.

On the following pages you will find many interesting and unusual types of dwellings for some of our common fur-bearing neighbors. Most of these were sketched on the spot or from photos I had taken previously. I visited some spots many times to get better acquainted with the creatures living there. Go out into the woods and find some neighbors of your own to watch and enjoy. It will surprise you to find just how thickly populated some of your "deserted" woods and fields really are.

One word of caution about any den, house, or burrow you may find. *Never* stick your hand or finger into any opening, no matter how small, and never enter any cave large enough to admit you. The owner might just be at home and he might also decide to fight for his privacy with tooth and claw.

If there are cobwebs across the doorway or if it is full of dead leaves, the dwelling is probably abandoned, but probe inside with a stick before you get closer. If there are flies buzzing about the opening or fresh tracks or other evidence in the immediate area, you may be pretty sure that there are tenants inside.

Look sharp and use caution, and animal "house hunting" can be an interesting and often exciting sort of safari!

TREE-HOLE DENS

Often you will find several holes in tree trunks and any or all of them may be lived in. But it is hard to tell who lives where, unless you can see the owner entering or leaving.

If the openings are small, 2 inches or less in diameter, the home may belong to a red squirrel, flying squirrel, or even a deer mouse (who loves to climb trees). If it is larger, 3 or 4 inches across, it may be the home of a gray squirrel, or a small owl, sparrow hawk, or woodpecker.

Flying squirrels like to make their dens in small holes close to the tops of trees or telephone poles. I know of one who lives in such a pole and I occasionally stop there, rap on the pole, and watch him sail out and across the road to another pole, where he promptly climbs to the top and gives me a fine bawling out.

If you find a tree with a hole or two, knock on the trunk with a stout stick or rock, and you may see the owner leaving in a hurry. However, don't do this too often or he will not return.

If you can climb up to inspect the opening, don't put your hand inside, but look for signs of wear and tear, or hairs about the opening, and be on the alert for the tenant's surprise departure. Occasionally even a snake will live in such a tree nest.

HOLLOW LOG DENS

Any hollow log may turn out to be the home of an animal, including, fox, rabbit, skunk, raccoon, or even a small bear. It depends on where you find the log, and the size of the opening into it.

If the log is near houses, it may belong to a skunk or a rabbit. If it is far from houses, yet still near civilization, it may be the home of a raccoon or fox as well. If you find a huge hollow log far out in the wilds, many miles from any type of civilization, it might also be the home of a small bear or bobcat.

Bits of bones, small skulls, feathers, or fur around the opening will tell you that this is the home of a carnivorous animal — a meat eater. In this case it is especially wise not to poke into it unless you are ready to beat a hasty retreat, if the dweller turns out to be a skunk or bobcat or a larger animal.

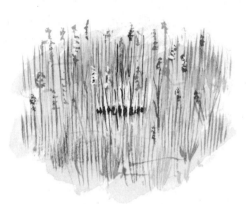

GROUND SQUIRREL BURROWS

There are several kinds of ground squirrels throughout the Midwest, particularly the thirteen-lined ground squirrel, which digs small burrows in lawns and prairies.

The burrow shown here was sketched in Rowan's Ravine, in Saskatchewan, Canada, near where I had camped. The little "gophers," as they are incorrectly called, always have one main entrance about 3 inches across and several escape hatches which they dive into when danger threatens.

The escape holes, as shown to the right in the sketch, have no dirt about them and, as they are small, they are hard to see in the grass. This makes them safer for the owners who can be a tenth of a second from safety down one of these holes.

If you find such a hole, look around for a radius of about 15 or 20 feet for the main hole and other escape hatches. If they are there, you have probably found a ground squirrel's home. The eastern chipmunk, who is a relative, occasionally lives in similar burrows although he usually prefers a refuge in a wall, log, or under a rock.

The ground squirrel's nest, often several feet underground, is lined with soft grasses and there are usually storerooms for vegetable matter which the ground squirrel stuffs away in short tunnels leading off the main one.

WOODCHUCK DEN

Like all burrowing animals, the woodchuck leaves a ring of dirt about the main entrance of his home. He also has one or two emergency, or escape, entrances hidden away in the tall grass or between the roots of a tree. These do not have any telltale piles of earth near them to reveal their presence.

The animal digs the escape tunnels from below, from the main tunnel or from his underground den, and carries the dirt out the main entrance. The woodchuck in the East and Southeast and the hoary marmot in the West dig similar burrows. The entrances are usually about 8 inches across.

Both these animals will build their dens in stone walls, in or under logs or rocks, or right out in the middle of a field. They can often be seen sitting up by the entrances to their dens or feeding nearby, never very far from one of the entrances. The openings are either vertical or horizontal. Occasionally a rabbit, skunk, or weasel will move into a woodchuck den after the owner has moved out.

Look for tracks in soft dirt by the entrance to help identify the present owner. If you find one of these dens near or in a clover field or vegetable garden, it is sure to belong to a woodchuck.

HARVEST MOUSE NEST

Once in a while you will find a small ball of woven grasses and reeds, about the size of a baseball, tucked away in a swamp or among the cattails along a pond bank. This is the home of the tiny harvest mouse.

These little seedeaters are found in greatest numbers in our Southeast and far West. They measure only about five inches long, half of which is tail.

The nests are very cleverly constructed and are usually either on the ground or a few inches above it, attached to cattails or other handy supports. In areas where the ground stays damp for long periods or there is much heavy rain, the little chaps are bound to build nests above where the water will reach.

Harvest mice raise several litters a year, so the nest is a very busy place as long as there are any of these little mice about. In the East, the harvest mice build their nests in thickets where seed-producing grasses and milkweed grow. If you find such a nest, keep an eye on it and if you are quiet you may see the owners.

66

BLACK BEAR DEN

This is a sketch of a black bear's den that I found on Panther Mountain in the Catskill Mountains of New York State. The bear had just left, for the den was still warm. It was dug under a big fallen beech tree and could hold three men with room to spare.

The bear had made a path to a nearby tree where he had scratched his back, and as high as I could reach there were black hairs caught in the bark, so he must have been a big animal.

Black bears make their hibernation dens in big fallen logs, in rock caves, or under such a log as this one. A Forest Service Ranger once told me that a party of skiers reported a large dead stump on fire, high on a western slope. He investigated and found that the "burning" stump had a bear hibernating inside and the "smoke" was steam from the bear's warm body.

In late fall you will frequently see, in bear country, where these big animals have tried to dig dens among rocks or stumps and then have gone away to find a better place. Their great strength enables them to move huge rocks with ease. If you ever find such a den and see steam coming from it, hear noises, or smell a strong odor from within, *do not disturb*, for, like most sleepers, bears are very grouchy when suddenly awakened. Look for tracks and/or droppings.

GRAY SQUIRREL NEST

As soon as the leaves fall off the trees in the fall, you will begin to see what look like huge bunches of leaves caught in high crotches of many trees. These are not birds' nests, or accidental collections of leaves. They are the nests of the gray squirrel in the East, and probably of the gray's relatives in the western portion of the country.

These nests are made during the spring and summer, and they may measure almost 2 feet in diameter. They are very cleverly constructed out of leaves, twigs, and small branches woven to-

68

gether so that they will stand high winds, hail, and the animal's constant going in and out. Even after hurricanes, you can still see many of these nests in good shape and ready for another occupant.

Some of the nests have been used for several years with new materials being added with each season. Other nests are abandoned after one season and left to the high winds.

Red squirrels also build leaf and twig nests, but they are usually on top of a limb and close to the trunk of the tree, not in a high crotch as shown here.

RED FOX DEN

The sleek and sly red fox can make his home in several places, but he seems to prefer a small cave or a burrow dug into a bank. If you find such a den and cannot decide if it was made by a fox or a woodchuck, look about the entrance to see if you find small bones, feathers, or bits of hair. If you discover any of these, the den belongs to a fox and not a "chuck," because the woodchuck is a vegetarian.

It is surprising how close to civilization and buildings you will find a fox's den. The one shown on page 69 is within a football-field length of my home, and although no one lives there at present, it has been lived in for several years. I have seen the owner many times when he didn't know I was watching him, and I have a hunch that he often watched me when I didn't know it either.

Foxes of all kinds dig burrows in banks, under logs, or even under outbuildings and barns. You can usually identify such dens by the litter about the entrance. Look for tracks, droppings, and flies about the doorway to be sure that it is lived in.

The red fox is found over most of the United States and far up into Canada. In the West, the gray fox and the kit or swift fox are found. All use similar dens. The red fox is also known as the cross fox, silver fox, or black fox, depending upon the color. Any of these colors can be found in a single litter of pups.

BEAVER HOUSE

These amazingly constructed houses used to be common over much of the northern portions of the United States, but the beaver has disappeared from a large part of his former range. Originally he was found all over the continental United States, except in a few arid areas and in Florida, but his valuable fur was his downfall, and trappers cut down his numbers considerably. He is still plentiful, often too much so, in portions of Canada and in some areas of our less-populated states, where his dams do damage by flooding.

Some beaver houses are 15 feet across and almost as high from the base to the vent at the top. They are entered from underwater and have a raised platform inside, above the water level, for living quarters, often divided into several rooms, some large enough for a man to crawl into.

The houses are strongly constructed of branches, twigs, and even small logs floated into position and woven into a compact dome over the living quarters. A man can safely climb on top of these houses, for they are rugged and sturdy. Look for them in small ponds above a beaver dam or in marshlands. The height of the dam is always designed to keep the entrances to the house covered with water but the living quarters high and dry. If the water level inside the beaver house begins to vary, the animal at once hurries to the dam to look for leaks. The houses are often plastered with mud for complete insulation, and when the mud freezes not even a bear could tear the house apart.

MINK DEN

When you are walking along a stream or a riverbank, look at the opposite bank to see if there are any small holes just above the waterline. If you see them, and signs of tracks leading down to the water, you have quite likely found the home of a mink.

These dens are about 4 inches in diameter and almost always close to water, often in the banks above it. Mink will also take up housekeeping in muskrat houses after the muskrat has been eaten by the new tenant. They can rip muskrat houses apart since they are made of grasses and small twigs, but they cannot harm a beaver house. They will also take over a woodchuck hole if it is close to water. They may even use a rock den or hollow stump as a home, but they seem to prefer a den of their own design as close as possible to water.

A mink den may consist of a tunnel into the bank as much as a dozen feet long, ending in a snug den lined with grasses and leaves. Occasionally there will also be an escape tunnel from the den into the water, away from the main entrance.

Although the dirt and refuse from a mink den usually fall into the water, look for signs of leftovers from meals on the bank above the entrance where this little member of the weasel family has eaten his meal. Look also for insects about the entrance, a sure sign that it has not been abandoned.

MUSKRAT HOUSE

You have probably seen these little mud and grass homes of the common muskrats in swamps and wetlands. They may be 4 or 5 feet across, or larger, and stand as much as 3 feet above the water. They can be distinguished from beaver houses because the muskrat does not use heavy sticks in the construction. Occasionally a few sticks are used but they are small so they can be woven with the grass roots and stalks combined with mud to form the house. The houses themselves are very much smaller than beaver houses.

They often have a small, well-used trail up to the top of the outside, where the owner will sit and bask in the sun with an eye out for danger.

The interior has a raised platform for living and usually one room for the family. The entrance is underwater, of course, where enemies cannot see the owner entering or leaving.

Besides the main house, there may be one or more smaller feeding shelters close by. These will be rounder and more uniform in shape and are merely used as resting shelters or for light snacks. The animals also use burrows in banks of streams and lakes, or among the roots of a bank-growing tree. If you find what looks like a big mink den, and there are bits of chewed plants and stems floating nearby, it is undoubtedly a muskrat den and not a mink's. If you find a small pile of chewed vegetation on a bank above a den, look carefully below it and you may find the opening of an escape tunnel.

RACCOON DEN

Being an expert tree climber, the raccoon prefers to have his den in an old tree, where there is an opening big enough for him to enter. This is usually where a large limb has rotted off, leaving a hole about 6 or 8 inches across. If you can reach it, you may see gray and brown hair caught in the bark of the opening. Look also at the tree bark below the opening for signs of hair.

Raccoons will use a hollow log on the ground for a den if no other spot can be found, or even an opening in a ledge, but if possible they will select a high hole in a big old tree, often using it for several years.

These dens are difficult to find. I feed several raccoons at my back door every night and have for several years, but so far I have never found their den. I have even backtracked them in winter to no avail. I do know that a couple of them live down a manhole in the highway in front of my house, but these "city folk" are an exception.

Tree dens are often preferred when the opening is sheltered by an overhanging branch or if the trunk of the tree slopes so that the opening is protected from rain and snow. When raccoons find such a snug home they move right in and often raise several families in the same comfortable homestead.

Keep an eye out for raccoon dens when you are walking in the woods, particularly if there are old trees with many broken limbs or split trunks.

COYOTE DEN

In areas where coyotes are plentiful, from the Gulf of Mexico to southern Canada, in some parts of Alaska, and as far east as New England, you may come across their dens in ledges, hollow logs, caves, or in burrows dug by the animal himself.

A burrow is usually under, or in, a soft sandy bank and has a characteristic semicircle of earth and rubble about the opening of the den. This opening may be 2 feet or more in diameter and usually there is plenty of refuse scattered about the area in front of the den.

If the den opening is much smaller, it may well be the home of a fox instead of a coyote, and, if the den is in the wilderness areas of our most northern states or Canada, it might also belong to a family of wolves. These dens do not have a secondary tunnel and entrance, for these animals have little to fear except man.

Often such a den as this one (page 77) that I sketched in Saskatchewan, Canada, will have a flattened area on the bank above it, where the adults have rested and watched their youngsters at play below them, or else just sunned themselves. Look carefully for tracks, animal hair, and bones about the den entrance, and keep an eye on the den from a distance with glasses. You may get to know an interesting family of "wild dogs."

RIVER OTTER DEN

Dens along the river or lake bank usually belong to the mink, muskrat, or the common otter. These dens were sketched less than

50 miles from New York City and were the homes of a pair of otters. They are larger than those of the mink or muskrat.

The bank was grassy all the way down to the water, and the triple doorways were almost hidden by the long grass. The den itself might be as much as 10 feet or more back into the bank and lined with sticks, leaves, and grass.

Most otter dens not only have above-water entrances in the bank but underwater escape tunnels as well. During the winter when the water is frozen, the animal will use the underwater entrance for his fishing trips under the ice, as well as the bank entrance for hunting trips above the frozen surface.

You may find traces of food scraps about the entrance, as well as the unusual tracks of this partially web-footed creature. If you find such a den and other signs that indicate an otter lives there, try to be patient and wait to see the animal itself. Otters are good-natured and love to play, so seeing them would be a fine experience for a young naturalist.

The sea otter is related to the river otter, but seldom builds similar dens. Their youngsters are often born in the water. Another relative, the cape otter of South Africa, is unique in that he has no claws at all, but just stubby "fingers."

DEER MOUSE NEST

It is always a surprise to see an animal do something you would never expect, and to see a little white-footed deer mouse scamper up a tree and disappear into a bird's nest can be quite startling.

These little chaps build nests in hollow trees, under building eaves, and in almost any high place, but one of their favorite homes is a bird's deserted nest with a neat little thatched roof of leaves. It does not make much difference what kind of nest it is to start with, for when the deer mouse is through with it, the nest is a snug little home, good for many nights of warm, sound sleep for the new tenant and family.

If you spot one of these split-level mouse nests, you may be able to catch a quick glimpse of the owner peeking out from under the newly installed roof, or adding a few leaves to his home.

PACK RAT NEST

If you ever come across a little pile of "rubbish" in the woods where the pack rat, or trade rat, lives, you have found a most unusual type of nest. Actually, museum might be a better word.

This little "shoplifter" will collect anything at all and bring it home to add to his nest pile. Near campgrounds where he has scampered about, you will find nests full of gum wrappers, paper clips, cartridge cases, car keys, pieces of combs, bobby pins, and almost any small thing. These trinkets are added to his collection with great glee, but the pack rat is a fair trader: he always leaves something in return — an acorn, leaf, twig, bit of bark, or perhaps a bit of crockery.

These animals are actually wood rats and there are several species. The name "pack rat" has been used for all of them with no distinction as to species, for they are all great swappers, or at least collectors, discarding nothing.

Pack rats are found, in one species or another, almost from coast to coast, but the western members of this clan particularly earn their name. Many youngsters who always collect things but never get rid of anything are often called "pack rats" by their parents. Perhaps your closets or bureau drawers resemble such a nest?

Droppings or Scat

Matter is never really destroyed, but merely changed in form. This is true of the food that our wild neighbors consume for their growth and life. Once the best parts have been absorbed for nourishment and growth, the residue is cast out.

This residue is dropped about the woodlands. From such droppings, or "scat" as naturalists call them, much can be learned as to who has been there, what they had found to eat, and how long ago.

Even a casual glance will tell the size of the animal who left the sign. The form and composition of the scat will frequently give further information as to the species of animal, hunting luck, and health. The scat of some species is unmistakable, and is, therefore, of great help in discovering the type of wildlife in an area.

Fresh scat is soft and dark in color while deposits made some days ago are light tan, gray, or white, much like sawdust or cigar ashes. Some contain finely chewed bits of grass and leaves, berry seeds, or fruit pits. Others, belonging to the meat eaters, contain bits of bone, fur, and feathers, identifying other animals in the area.

A study of the scat of animals will add much to your knowledge of wildlife. Sherlock Holmes, the famed fictional detective, could tell much about a criminal by the ashes of his cigar; so, too, can a naturalist tell much about animals from the "ashes" of their meals. This is an important sign not to be overlooked.

RABBIT

The scat of all rabbits and hares are distinctive, and there is never any question as to whether or not a rabbit or hare left them. They are invariably almost round or egg-shaped and appear to be made of fine sawdust pressed into small balls. The individual pellets may be flattened on the sides.

The color, when fresh, may be a dark green or greenish brown, depending upon the diet of the particular animal. They soon dry out and, after a few days, will be light tan or almost white in color.

The composition is finely chopped and digested shreds and bits of grass eaten by the animal, and the size of the pellets vary from about $\frac{5}{16}$ inch in diameter, for those of the eastern cottontail rabbit, to about $\frac{1}{2}$ inch for those of the arctic hare.

There may be from a half dozen to two dozen pellets in a deposit, and they soon disintegrate in rain and become fertilizer. Look for this type of scat along garden paths; near burrows; in patches of clover; in briar patches; hollow logs; brush tangles; and near where you have surprised rabbits or hares.

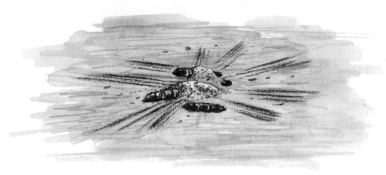

BOBCAT

All members of the cat and dog family try to cover up their droppings so as not to reveal their presence to a possible enemy. Perhaps you have noticed your own cat or dog attempting to do this.

Cats also occasionally dig a small hole for the droppings and then cover up the hole. In the wilds this is not always possible but the scat of such felines as bobcat, lynx, and mountain lion will very frequently be at least partially concealed. Look for scratch marks.

The size of the segments depends upon the size of the animal. If you are in wilderness areas where lions are known to be found and the diameter of the sections is an inch or more, you may be sure lions *are* about. If the sign is found in deep woods where small game is plentiful and there are no houses about to shelter a tame tabby, you can be pretty sure that it is a bobcat, or (if in Canada or some portions of our northern states) a lynx. These animals leave a much smaller scat, with the segments measuring about ½ inch in diameter.

If any sign of a hole having been dug is present, you may be positive that some kind of feline has been there. When fresh, the scat is brown or almost black, but soon turns gray and finally chalky. Look near dens, hollow logs, fresh kills, or flattened areas of grass where the cat has been sunning himself.

GRAY SQUIRREL

Many small animals — squirrels, rats and mice, gophers, etc. — all leave droppings of about the same size and construction, and the scat of one of my neighborly gray squirrels, as sketched, could as well be that of a dozen different animals of the same size.

About the only information given to a naturalist by such scat is that some small-sized animal is in the area. Smaller animals leave droppings the size of that of the house mouse, probably familiar to most of you. This includes field mice and voles of assorted species.

Look for such small signs on stone walls, near dens or burrows or small hollow logs, or near where there may be seed-bearing plants.

Such droppings are usually composed of extremely fine bits of grass, nutmeats, and seeds. When they have dried, they appear to be made of extremely fine sawdust. The segment sizes may range from 1/4 inch to 1/2 inch in length, and the diameter from 1/8 inch for the voles and mice, and up to 1/4 inch for squirrels.

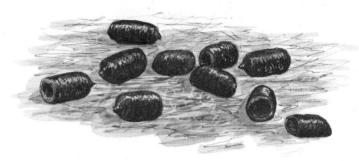

DEER

Some summers ago when a city family rented a nearby house, they were always calling me up to ask questions about things in nature that they had seen, heard, or found. One day I received a frantic call to come and see a nest full of "black-snake's eggs" that they had found in the garden. This I had to see for myself!

When I got there a few moments later I found them gathered around a fresh deposit of white-tailed deer droppings in their vegetable garden. They were much disappointed that they were not snake eggs, but delighted to know that real live deer were that close to their house.

Deer scat, when fresh, is usually shiny dark green or black, depending upon what kinds of vegetation the deer have been eating. It dries and bleaches out in a few days to a light brown or gray and finally, with rain, disintegrates and vanishes.

The segments average about $5/8$ inch in diameter and about $3/4$ inch or an inch in length. Look for them near gardens, along deer runs, near flattened-down grassy "deer beds" where deer have been resting or sleeping, or in apple orchards — a favorite place for deer to feed.

All members of the deer family have similar scat, so knowledge of the species in the area where the sign is found will help you to determine what kind of animals are living nearby.

RACCOON

The scat of some animals or the characteristics of the material make identification quite easy, and the scat of the raccoon is a sign which can usually be positively identified.

This animal has the peculiar habit of depositing its scat on top of big logs, limbs, or rocks. If you find scat on such things as fallen timber, low heavy branches, or rocks, you may be sure that one of our black-masked neighbors has been around.

The scat of the raccoon is varied in color, depending upon diet, and ranges from black to reddish, soon bleaching out to gray, resembling a cigar ash in color and texture. It may contain fruit seeds and bits of bone, as the animal eats both vegetable matter and meat.

The sections are about ½ inch in diameter, and the segments may be either flat-ended or tapered. Look for them near cornfields, fruit orchards, or nut trees and along river and stream banks where these interesting chaps go to fish for crayfish and frogs.

BLACK BEAR

Black-bear scat can contain the greatest variety of materials due to the bear's wide diet. As he is not a strict vegetarian but will eat meat upon occasion, or carrion (meat from animals already dead), the droppings may include scraps of fur; berry seeds; bits of bone, wood, and insect shells; nut husks; fish scales; and about anything else that is edible.

The segments may be cleanly broken and comparatively dry in composition, or smooth, tapered, and soft in structure, depending upon the diet. All bleach out eventually into a dry crumbly gray or white material.

The size of the scat varies with the animal but is generably an inch or more in diameter, while the sections will vary in length. The scat of all members of the bear family are similar, so you must be governed by the species of bear known to be in the area where the sign is found.

You may find scat along animal runs, in orchards, berry patches, near beds of wild strawberries (a favorite fruit of the bear), or along streams where the animal has gone to fish. Dumps and garbage areas near resorts or camps are places where this scat may be found quite frequently. If you find fresh bear scat, move about with care as the bear may still be in the area. You might be able to catch a fleeting glimpse of him before he sees you.

88

Index

C. B. COLBY has more than eighty books to his credit; a third of them dealing with the outdoors, camping, conservation, or wildlife. His books are most popular items with boys on young readers' shelves in libraries across the country.

Ever since he was a boy himself in New Hampshire, Mr. Colby has been interested in the outdoors and wildlife. Perhaps the fact that he knows the outdoors firsthand as well as the animals who live there is what makes him one of the most popular nature authors for young people.

For nearly eight years he was a Special Game Protector for the State of New York, and since 1958 has been Camping Editor of *Outdoor Life* magazine. He is the only American to be appointed "Surveillant Auxiliaire" (Auxiliary Warden) of the vast and beautiful Mont Tremblant Park in Quebec Province, Canada, and also has the distinction of having a small lake named after him there. (It is called Lac Colibi, French for Lake Colby.)

His hobbies include hunting, fishing, camping, photography, illustration (he graduated from art school in 1925), and taping wildlife sounds for use in lectures. He is a member and director of the Outdoor Writers Association of America, a member of The Camp Fire Club of America and of the Adventurers Club of New York. He is married and has two grown children.

When not away on a research or speaking trip, the author lives in Briarcliff Manor, New York, where he does his writing and illustrating. However, many of his sketches for *The First Book of Animal Signs* were made right in the wilderness where the signs were found.